# CIARA

Gareth Stevens
Publishing

By Maeve Griffin

**Please visit our website, www.garethstevens.com. For a free color catalog of all our high-quality books, call toll free 1-800-542-2595 or fax 1-877-542-2596.**

Library of Congress Cataloging-in-Publication Data

Griffin, Maeve.
Ciara / Maeve Griffin.
    p. cm. — (Hip-hop headliners)
Includes bibliographical references and index.
ISBN 978-1-4339-6602-6 (pbk.)
ISBN 978-1-4339-6603-3 (6-pack)
ISBN 978-1-4339-6600-2 (library binding)
1.  Ciara (Vocalist)—Juvenile literature. 2.  Singers—United States—Biography—Juvenile literature.  I. Title.
ML3930.C47G75 2012
782.42164092—dc23
[B]
                                    2011018200

First Edition

Published in 2012 by
**Gareth Stevens Publishing**
111 East 14th Street, Suite 349
New York, NY 10003

Designer: Haley W. Harasymiw
Editor: Therese M. Shea

Photo credits: Cover background Shutterstock.com; cover, p. 1 (Ciara) John Shearer/ WireImage/Getty Images; p. 5 Ethan Miller/Getty Images; p. 7 Jason Kempin/Getty Images; p. 9 Kevin C. Cox/Getty Images; p. 11 Raymond Boyd/Getty Images; p. 13 Matt Jolonek/ Getty Images; p. 15 Peter Kramer/Getty Images; p. 17 Jamie McCarthy/WireImage/Getty Images; p. 19 Kevin Winter/Getty Images; p. 21 Joe Scarnici/Stringer/Getty Images; p. 23 Robyn Beck/Getty Images; p. 25 Joe Corrigan/Stringer/Getty Images; pp. 27, 29 Stephen Lovekin/Getty Images.

Printed in the United States of America

CPSIA compliance information: Batch #CW12GS: For further information contact Gareth Stevens, New York, New York at 1-800-542-2595.

# Contents

# Hip-Hop Princess

Ciara is called a hip-hop princess. Her music has a strong beat. It is fun to dance to.

# Young Traveler

Ciara was born in Austin, Texas, on October 25, 1985. Her full name is Ciara Princess Harris.

Ciara's father was in the US Army. The family lived in Germany, New York, Utah, California, Arizona, and Nevada. Finally, they settled in Atlanta, Georgia.

# The Goal

Young Ciara loved the music of Destiny's Child and Janet Jackson. When she was a teen, she wrote a goal on a piece of paper. She wanted to be a singer.

Ciara joined an all-girl music group called Hearsay. She also wrote songs on her own.

13

## First Album

After high school, Ciara worked for a record company called LaFace Records. Many hip-hop stars helped her with her first album, including Lil Jon.

Ciara's first hit song, "Goodies," topped the music charts in 2004. Her songs with Missy Elliott and Ludacris were big hits, too.

Missy Elliott

17

## More Albums

In 2005, Ciara went on tour with
Gwen Stefani. She went on tour
with Bow Wow in 2006. Her second
album, *The Evolution*, came out
later that year. It was a top-selling
hip-hop album.

Bow Wow

Ciara's third album was called *Fantasy Ride*. She worked on it with more hip-hop stars, including Young Jeezy, Tricky Stewart, and The-Dream.

Tricky Stewart

The-Dream

21

Ciara loved working with The-Dream. They worked together on her fourth album, *Basic Instinct*. It came out in 2010.

23

# A Big Honor

Ciara was named Woman of the Year in 2008 by the Billboard music business. She was honored as a leader in music.

25

## More Goals

Ciara has reached other goals, too. She wanted to be a model. She is now a model. Ciara wanted to act. She has acted in several movies.

Ciara has a new goal. Someday, she wants to make clothes for her fans to wear. What will Ciara do next?

# Timeline

**1985**    Ciara is born on October 25 in Austin, Texas.

**2003**    Ciara begins to work with LaFace Records.

**2004**    Ciara's first album comes out.

**2005**    Ciara goes on tour with Gwen Stefani.

**2006**    *The Evolution* comes out.

**2008**    Ciara is named Billboard's Woman of the Year.

**2009**    *Fantasy Ride* comes out.

**2010**    *Basic Instinct* comes out.

# For More Information

## Books

Leavitt, Amie Jane. *Ciara*. Hockessin, DE: Mitchell Lane Publishers, 2008.

Simone, Jacquelyn. *Ciara*. Broomall, PA: Mason Crest, 2008.

## Websites

### Ciara

*www.billboard.com/artist/ciara/617021*

Read more about Ciara's life and albums.

### Ciara

*www.ciaraworld.com/us*

Find out if Ciara is on tour near you.

**Publisher's note to educators and parents:** Our editors have carefully reviewed these websites to ensure that they are suitable for students. Many websites change frequently, however, and we cannot guarantee that a site's future contents will continue to meet our high standards of quality and educational value. Be advised that students should be closely supervised whenever they access the Internet.

## Glossary

**goal:** something important someone wants to do

**model:** one who is paid to wear clothes or goods for others to see

**record:** a copy of music that can be played again and again

**tour:** a trip to many places in order to sing and play music for people

## Index